Hamsters

Julie Murray

Abdo
FAMILY PETS
Kids

abdopublishing.com

Published by Abdo Kids, a division of ABDO, PO Box 398166, Minneapolis, Minnesota 55439.
Copyright © 2016 by Abdo Consulting Group, Inc. International copyrights reserved in all countries.
No part of this book may be reproduced in any form without written permission from the publisher.

Printed in the United States of America, North Mankato, Minnesota.

052015

092015

THIS BOOK CONTAINS
RECYCLED MATERIALS

Photo Credits: Corbis, Glow Images, iStock, Minden Pictures, Shutterstock

Production Contributors: Teddy Borth, Jennie Forsberg, Grace Hansen

Design Contributors: Candice Keimig, Dorothy Toth

Library of Congress Control Number: 2014958424

Cataloging-in-Publication Data

Murray, Julie.

 Hamsters / Julie Murray.

  p. cm. -- (Family pets)

ISBN 978-1-62970-902-4

Includes index.

1. Hamsters--Juvenile literature. 2. Pets--Juvenile literature.   I. Title.

636.935'6--dc23

                2014958424

Table of Contents

Hamsters

Hamsters make great
family pets.

They are small and soft.

Kate holds her hamster.

They like to live alone.
They may fight with
other hamsters.

Hamsters need a cage.

It has to be kept clean.

They need soft **bedding**.

It keeps them warm.

Hamsters like to **chew**.

Small sticks work well.

They need food.

They need water.

They need a wheel to run on.

They need a place to hide.

Is a hamster the right pet for your family?

Hamster Supplies

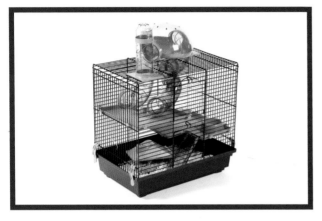

cage

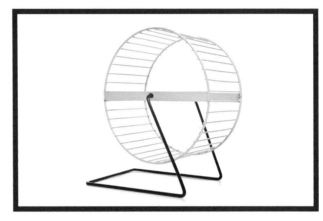

hamster wheel

food

water dispenser

Glossary

bedding
a material, usually wood shavings, put on the bottom of a hamster's cage for comfort and to keep the cage clean.

chew
to bite over and over.

Index

abdokids.com

Use this code to log on to abdokids.com and access crafts, games, videos, and more!

Abdo Kids Code:
FHK9024